Dirt Simple Uke

by Joe Carr

Audio Contents

<table>
<tr><td colspan="2">Track #</td><td colspan="2">Track #</td></tr>
<tr><td>1</td><td>Tuning</td><td>11</td><td>Old Joe Clark</td></tr>
<tr><td>2</td><td>The C6 Chord</td><td>12</td><td>Roll in My Sweet Baby's Arms</td></tr>
<tr><td>3</td><td>Row, Row, Row Your Boat</td><td>13</td><td>Strum Rhythms 1</td></tr>
<tr><td>4</td><td>The C6 Blues</td><td>14</td><td>Strum Rhythms 2</td></tr>
<tr><td>5</td><td>Mary Had a Little Lamb</td><td>15</td><td>Worried Man Blues</td></tr>
<tr><td>6</td><td>Skip to My Lou</td><td>16</td><td>The Sloop John B.</td></tr>
<tr><td>7</td><td>Twinkle, Twinkle Little Star</td><td>17</td><td>Columbus Stockade Blues</td></tr>
<tr><td>8</td><td>Amazing Grace</td><td>18</td><td>House of the Rising Sun</td></tr>
<tr><td>9</td><td>On Top of Old Smokey</td><td>19</td><td>Grandfather's Clock</td></tr>
<tr><td>10</td><td>B-I-N-G-O</td><td>20</td><td>The Midnight Special</td></tr>
</table>

Special thanks to Gerald Jones for his playing on the accompanying CD.
Tenor ukulele by Joe Mendel of Mendel Fretted Instruments, Chesterfield, MO.

1 2

Visit us on the Web at www.melbay.com — E-mail us at email@melbay.com

Contents

Dirt Simple Ukulele

The ukulele is a great choice for those who may feel challenged by other stringed instruments. Almost immediately, the beginner can start strumming and have fun making music. The music and instruction here are designed for those with little or no previous musical experience.

Each arrangement includes guitar chords that can be played as accompaniment. The given music is correct for soprano, concert and tenor ukuleles tuned in the re-entrant style to G C E A. This music can also be played on baritone ukulele, but the music will sound in a different key and the guitar chords will not be correct.

Re-entrant refers to the order of notes in the standard "my dog has fleas" ukulele tuning. Instead of ascending low to high, the uke tuning begins with a G note followed by a lower C note. If a player chooses to replace the fourth string with a thicker string and tune it to the G one octave lower than normal, this is referred to as "low G" tuning and the uke tuning then is no longer considered re-entrant. This is a possible but less common way to tune the uke.

Careful tuning is an important part of achieving a good sound. Use CD track 1 to get in good tune before each playing session. If you prefer to use a keyboard, tune the strings to G C E A (Green Cows Eat Apples.) For experienced guitarists, these strings are like the 4th through 1st strings of the guitar capoed at the 5th fret. Alternately, the familiar tune "my dog has fleas" can be used to tune if no standard note source is available. When using this "by ear" method, be careful that the C string is not too loose (bad sound) and the A string is not too tight (it may break.)

Track 1

The C6 Chord

When all 4 of the ukulele's strings are strummed together, they produce a C6 chord. Opposite is a double staff with standard music notation at the top and a tablature staff on the bottom. Notice there are 4 lines in the tablature staff. These lines represent the 4 strings of the ukulele. The lowest string on the staff is the 4th string or the closest to your face as you hold the ukulele in playing position. The top string on the staff is the 1st string or the closest string to the floor as you hold the ukulele in playing position. The numbers on the lines indicate at which fret each string should be fretted, the zeros on the staff mean the strings should be played "open" or without left-hand fingers touching the strings. Listen to track 2 and strum along, counting to 4 over and over.

Track 2

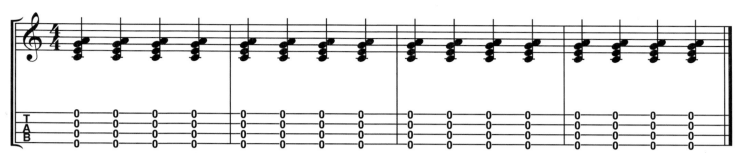

Row, Row, Row Your Boat

Here is a familiar song that can be played using only the C6 chord! Strum along with the CD track counting to 4 over and over. Use the fleshy pad of the right hand thumb for strumming and strive to brush across the tops of the strings in a smooth motion. If your thumb gets caught in the strings, you are digging down too hard.

Practice brushing lightly over the top of the strings. As you get comfortable with this basic brush strum, you can slowly begin to strum with more force and increase the volume.

Row, row, row your boat, gent-ly down the stream.   Mer-ri-ly, mer-ri-ly, mer-ri-ly, mer-ri-ly,   life is but a dream.

Chord Diagrams

Here is a diagram of the C6 chord. The zeros above the strings indicate unfretted, open strings. Later diagrams will have dots on the strings indicating where the left-hand fingers should fret the strings.

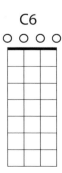

C6

The C6 Blues

The C6 Blues begins with the chord we learned above. The F6/9 chord shown in measure 2 requires a technique called the barre. Lay the left-hand 3rd finger (ring) flat across the 1st, 2nd and 3rd strings at the 5th fret. Pick each string separately, making sure each note sounds clearly with no buzzes. You may have to adjust your finger pressure or angle until the sound is good. The G6 chord in measure 9 is fretted the same way. When you are comfortable with the chords, try playing along with the CD track. The basic blues form is very common and it is important to know it well.

Track 4

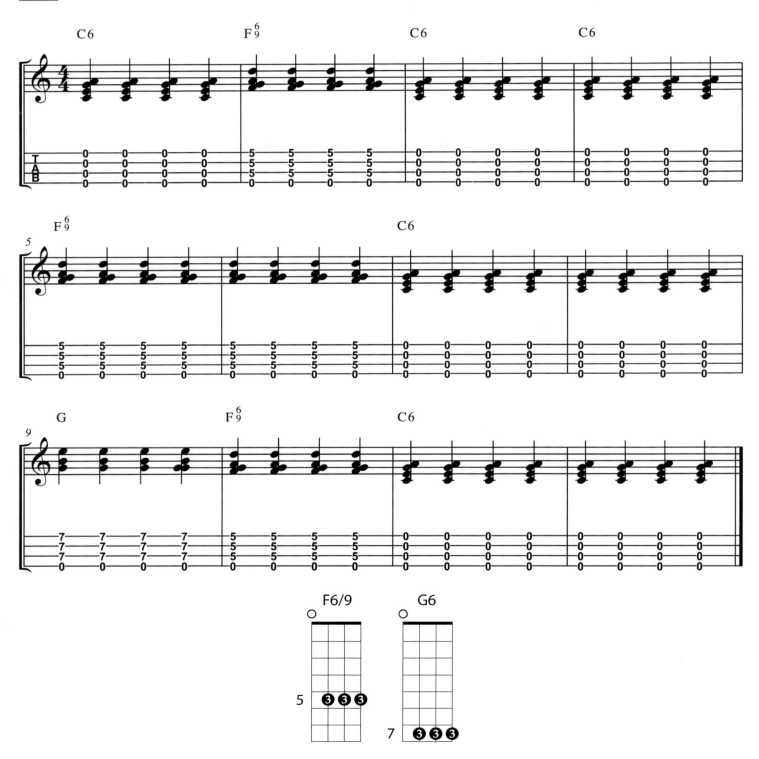

Mary Had a Little Lamb

This 2 chord song introduces new changing chords in time with music. It is in the key of F, so we will need 2 chords: F and C7. Study the diagrams below and practice these new forms. Use your index (1) and middle (2) fingers to form the F chord. Make sure to curve the fingers so they don't interfere with the open second string. Pick each string separately, listening for a clear tone.

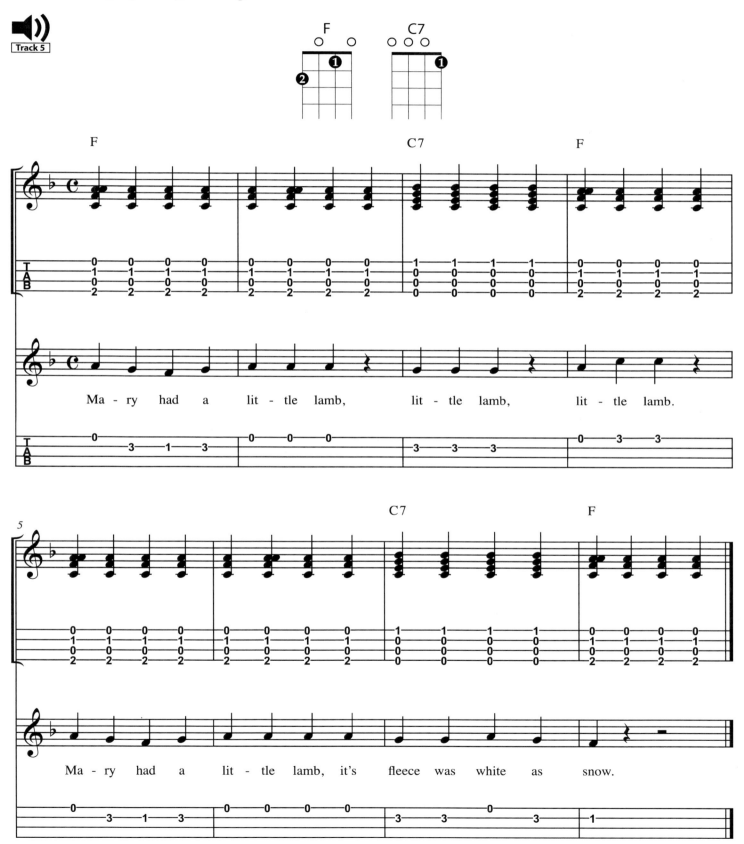

Skip To My Lou

Here is another 2 chord song in F.

Skip, skip, skip to my lou. Skip, skip, skip to my lou. Skip, skip,

skip to my lou. Skip to my lou my dar - ling.

Twinkle, Twinkle Little Star

Here is a familiar song with 3 chords. The B♭ chord requires a barre with the 1st finger at the 1st fret of the 1st and 2nd strings. Be sure that both barred strings sound clearly.

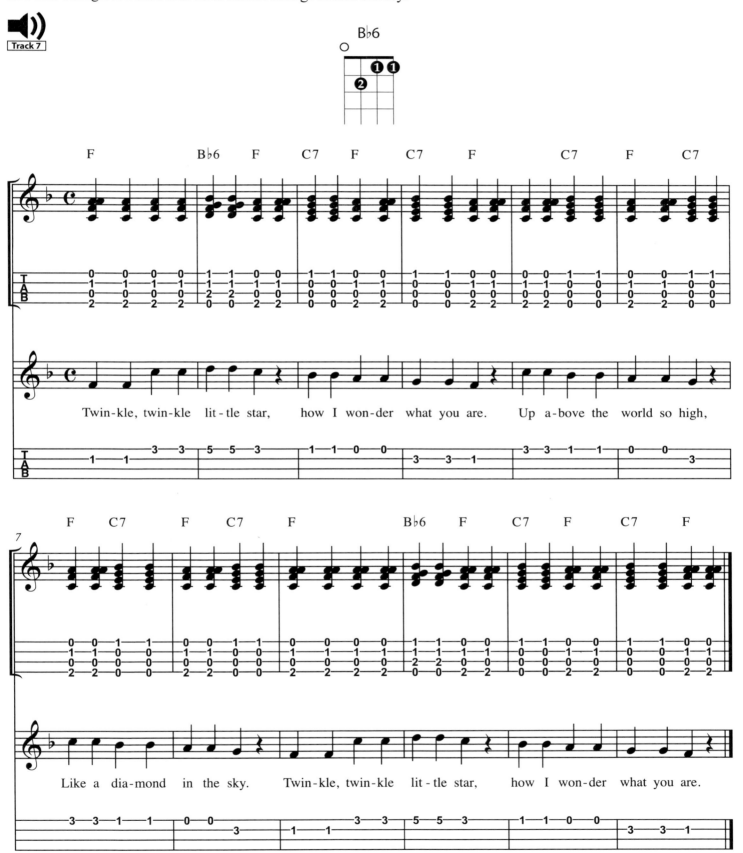

Amazing Grace

This well known song is in 3/4 or waltz time. There are 3 beats in each measure and we count 1-2-3-1-2-3 as we play it. Instead of 4 strums, there are only 3 per measure. It may take several minutes of concentration to change to 3/4 time from 4/4 time. Try playing the 1st measure repeatedly to get the correct feel.

Track 8

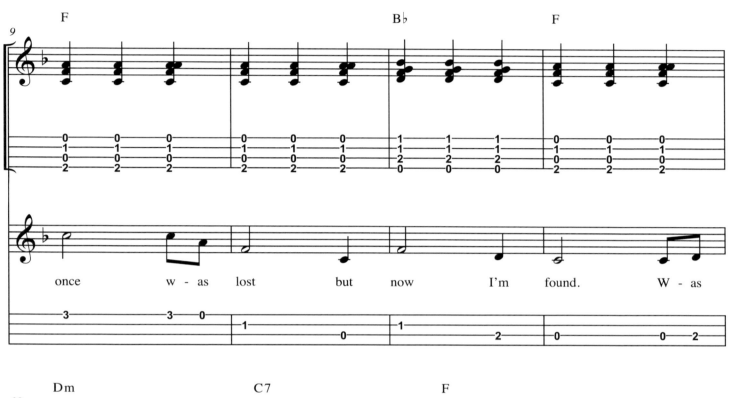

once   w - as   lost   but   now   I'm   found.   W - as

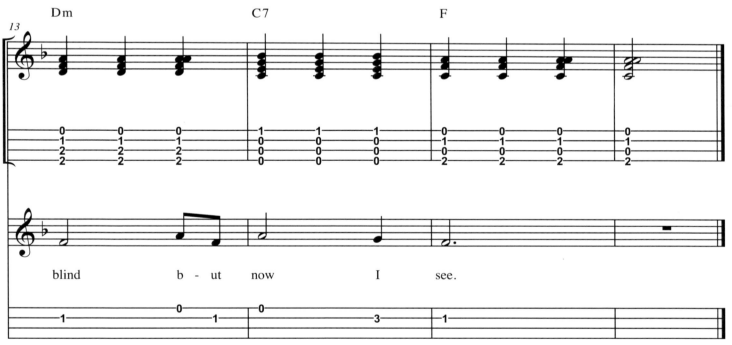

blind   b - ut   now   I   see.

On Top of Old Smokey

Here is another song in 3/4 time. Children often sing the parody "On Top of Spaghetti." Note the new chord forms.

On top of old Smo - key, All co - vered with snow.

I lost my tru lov - er, by cour-ting too slow.

B-I-N-G-O

This popular camp song introduces several new chords.

Track 10

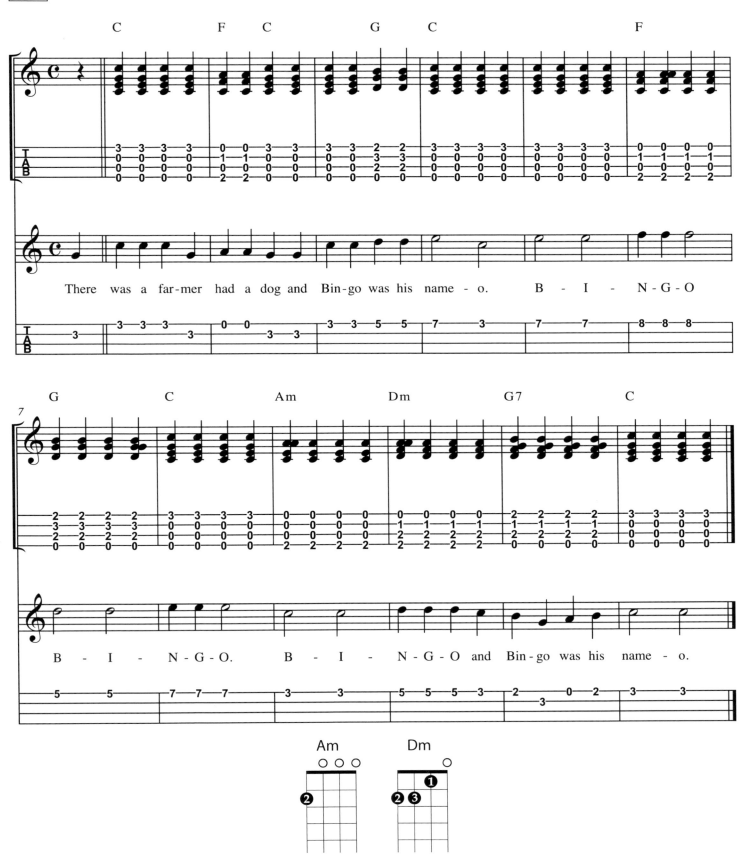

Old Joe Clark

This 2 chord song is in the key of D. The D chord is best played using the indicated fingering with the 1, 2 and 3 fingers forming a small triangle. When making the chord at first, place the 1st finger before the others.

Track 11

Six - teen miles of moun - tain road, six - teen miles of sand.

Ev - er I trav - el this road a - gain I'll be a mar - ried man.

Roll in My Sweet Baby's Arms

This song introduces a new strumming pattern. Count: 1 2+ 3+ 4+. Beat one is played with a downstroke while 2+ is played down-up. The entire measure then is played down, down-up, down-up, down-up. Listen to the CD track and practice measure 1 before trying the whole song.

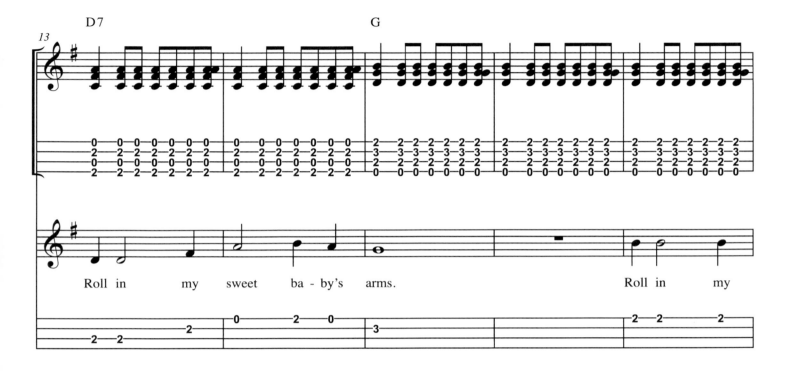

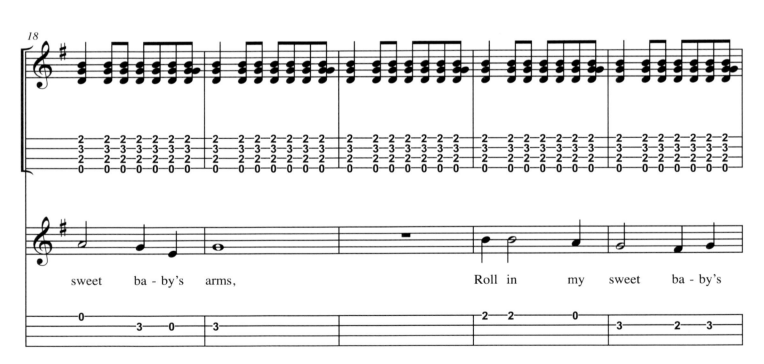

arms. Gon - na lay a-round the shack 'til the mail train comes

back and I'll roll in my sweet ba - by's arms.

Strum Rhythms 1

The basic rhythm in 4/4 time was presented as 4 quarter note downstrokes per measure as shown in measure 1. The marks above the measure represent downstrokes. In measure 2, there are eight eighth notes. They are played with alternating down-up down-up strokes. The "V" marks above the measure indicates the up strokes. While down strokes are strummed through all four strings, up strokes should only brush 2 or occasionally 3 strings. While many players use their thumb on both the down and up stroke, some prefer to use the index finger of the right hand to brush upwards over the strings.

Track 13

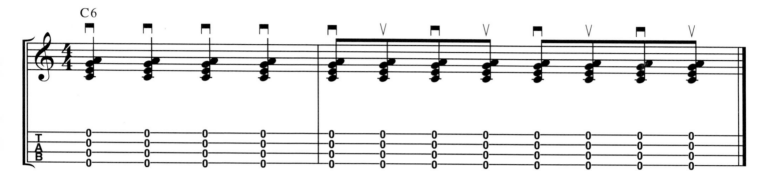

Strum Rhythms 2

The basic rhythm in measure 1 below is called the single shuffle borrowed from the name of a fiddle bowing. The pattern is down, down up, down, down up. Listen carefully to the audio for guidance. The advanced rhythm in measure 2 below uses upstrokes on the up beats. The measure counts 1+2 +3 + 4+

P P P P PP

The "P"s indicate the 5 pickstrokes in the measure. The pick direction is down up, up, up, down up. Again, listen carefully to the audio.

Track 14

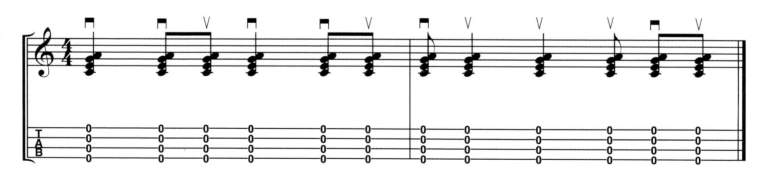

Worried Man Blues

This traditional blues is accompanied with single shuffle rhythm.

Track 15

It takes a wor - ried man to sing a wor - ried song. It

takes a wor - ried man to sing a wor - ried song. It

takes   a   wor - ried   man   to   sing   a   wor - ried   song   I'm   wor - ried

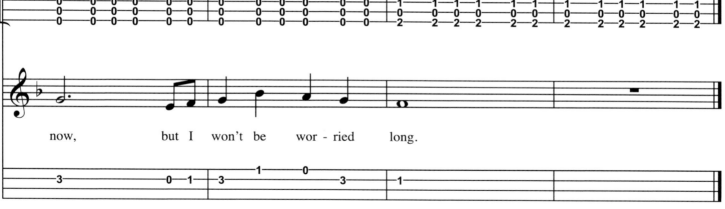

now,   but I   won't be   wor - ried   long.

The Sloop John B.

This song was written around 1900 about a ship in the Caribbean. Review page 17 for information on the strum pattern.

Track 16

Columbus Stockade Blues

This traditional blues has been recorded by many performers.

ade   friends   all   turned their back on me.   Go   and

leave me   if you wish   to.   Nev - er let it   cross your mind.

House of the Rising Sun

"Rising Sun Blues" may have originally been about a brothel in England. Americans made it about a similar establishment in New Orleans. A successful version was recorded by the English rock group The Animals in 1964.

Track 18

Grandfather's Clock

This popular song was written by Henry Clay Work in 1876.

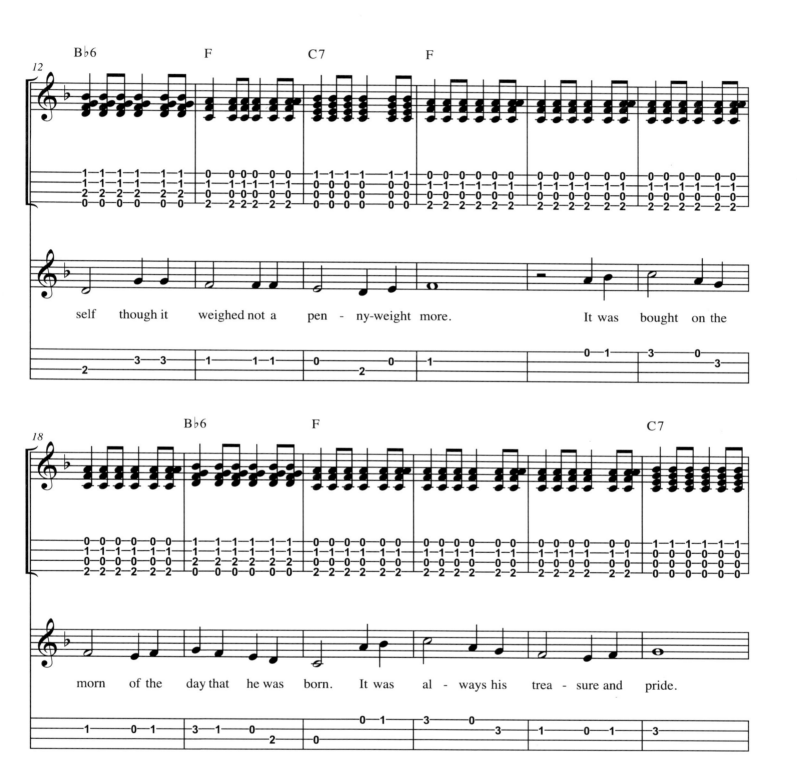

self though it weighed not a pen - ny-weight more. It was bought on the

morn of the day that he was born. It was al - ways his trea - sure and pride.

But it stopped, short, nev-er to run a - gain when the old

man died. Nine-ty years with-out slum-ber - ing, tic tock

The Midnight Special

A traditional song about a train and a prisoner.

Wake up in the morn - ing hear the ding dong ring.

Look out on the ta - ble, see the same old thing. Let the Mid - night

Conclusion

Congratulations! By completing this volume you are well on your way to strumming fun. There are many song books and Internet sites with words and chords to thousands of songs. With the basic chords and strums in this volume, you will be able to play much of this material.

Be sure to look for other Mel Bay Ukulele books including *Great Melodies for Solo Ukulele, Gospel Songs for Solo Ukulele, Holiday Favorites for Solo Ukulele, Folk Songs for Solo Ukulele,* and *Ukulele for Seniors* by Joe Carr.

About the Author

Since 1985, Joe Carr has been a music instructor specializing in Bluegrass, Western Swing and Irish music in the Commercial Music program at South Plains College in Levelland, Texas. He is a director for Camp Bluegrass, a summer residential Music camp in its 26th year (2012).

In 1977, Joe joined the internationally known *Country Gazette* bluegrass band with banjo player Alan Munde and bluegrass legend Roland White. Joe appeared on three group albums, a solo album and numerous other recorded projects during his seven-year tenure with the band. In the 1990s, Carr and Munde formed a duo that toured extensively throughout the U.S., Canada and England and recorded two albums for Flying Fish/Rounder Records.

Joe has developed and appeared in over thirty instructional music videos for Mel Bay Publications and Texas Music & Video. He has written many instructional book/CD combinations for Mel Bay and has a growing number of DVDs available. Included are diverse titles such as *Western Swing Fiddle* MB20289BCD, *Mandolin Gospel Tunes* MB20554BCD and *School of Country Guitar* MB21645BCD.

Joe is a regular columnist for *Flatpicking Guitar Magazine* and *Mandolin Magazine*. In 1996, the Texas Tech University Press published *Prairie Nights to Neon Lights: The Story of Country Music in West Texas* by Carr and Munde. Joe can be seen and heard at acousticmusician.com/JoeCarr.html. Joe plays Joe Mendel ukuleles.